turned on or before

Contributory Author
Brian Knapp, BSc, PhD
Art Director
Duncan McCrae, BSc
Special photography
Graham Servante
Special models
Tim Fulford, MA, Head of Design and Technology,
Leighton Park School
Editorial consultants
Anna Grayson, Rita Owen
Science advisor
Jack Brettle, BSc, PhD, Chief Research Scientist,
Pilkington plc
Production controller
Gillian Gatehouse
Print consultants
Landmark Production Consultants Ltd
Printed and bound in Hong Kong
Produced by *EARTHSCAPE EDITIONS*

First published in the United Kingdom in 1991
by Atlantic Europe Publishing Company Limited
86 Peppard Road, Sonning Common, Reading,
Berkshire, RG4 9RP, UK
Tel: (0734) 723751   Fax: (0734) 724488

Copyright © 1991
Atlantic Europe Publishing Company Limited

Reprinted in 1992

British Library Cataloguing in Publication Data
Knapp, Brian
    How things work
    1. Technology – For children
    I. Title   II. Series
    600

        ISBN 1-869860-85-3

01444
- Ref 600

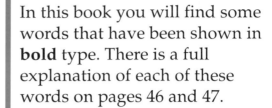

In this book you will find some words that have been shown in **bold** type. There is a full explanation of each of these words on pages 46 and 47.

On many pages you will find experiments that you might like to try for yourself. They have been put in a coloured box like this.

Acknowledgements
The publishers would like to thank the following:
Micklands Primary School, Redlands County
Primary School and Duncan Cooper.

Picture credits
t=top b= bottom l=left r=right

All photographs from the Earthscape Editions
photographic library except the following:
Miele 41b

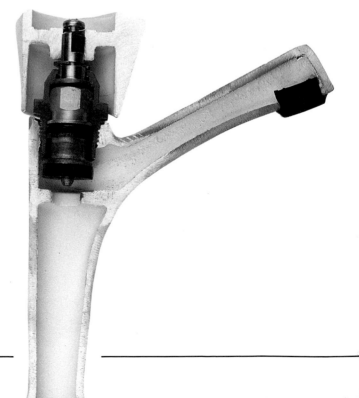

Contents

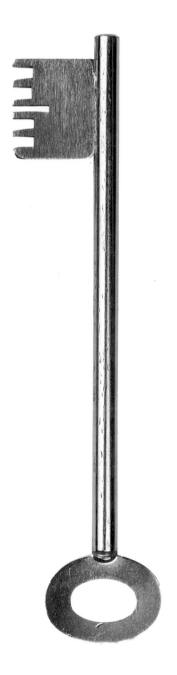

Introduction

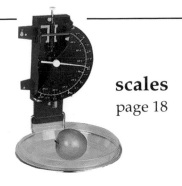

scales
page 18

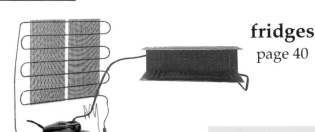

fridges
page 40

calculator
page 28

coolers
page 42

corkscrew
page 32

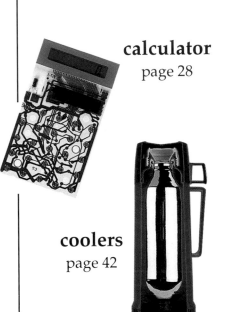

Look around. You live in a world of tools and machines. Your hair has been cut by a tool, your clothes have been made by a machine, your food has been cooked by a machine.

Tools and machines make our world a more comfortable place to live, they save us time and effort, and they can do many of the things we are unable to do ourselves.

Since earliest times people have been designing machines. Over the centuries many simple ideas have been gradually changed from their first simple design. For example, the knife that was once used to cut grain at harvest time has been developed into a combine harvester (a harvester, sorter and

lifters
page 30

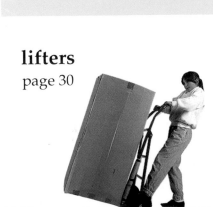

heater
page 44

vacuum
page 26

openers
page 12

cutter
page 8

pen
page 14

siphon
page 22

plugs
page 36

lamp
page 34

seed bagger put into one super machine). The fire that came by rubbing sticks together has been developed into a nuclear reactor. The cupped hands used to shout into the distance has become a telephone.

We live in a very exciting age. But no matter how complicated a machine might seem on the outside, it usually uses a simple idea somewhere on the inside. In this book we will look at some of the tools and machines you use every day, sometimes by taking them apart and showing you what is normally hidden from view.

Find out about tools and machines in any way you choose. Just turn to a page and make your discoveries.

lock
page 10

bells
page 38

spray
page 20

binoculars
page 24

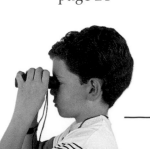

zip
page 16

catches
page 6

Catches and closers

A catch holds something closed. There are many types of catches, some of which work like levers, making easy work out of a hard job. Others use **magnets** and some even use springs.

Pressing the bar **pivots** the catch around this point and raises the other end of the bar out of the slot

A door latch
This kind of latch is designed to hold a door firmly closed. It is a simple type of lock. It cannot be opened unless the lever is lifted out of a slot in the door frame.

This end of the bar goes into a slot on the door frame

This end of the bar has a thumb place to make it easy to press

6

Spring catch

This is used for cupboards and doors where a strong catch is not needed. As a door is closed the roller meets the door frame and it is forced back into its slot. This compresses the spring. The spring holds the roller against the door frame. Sometimes the roller fits into a specially made cup-shaped hollow in the door frame.

The strength of the catch depends on the strength of the spring and whether or not there is a hollow on the door frame.

A spring catch

As the door is pushed shut the roller moves up the side of the hole and makes the spring shorter

The pressure of the spring holds the roller against the door frame and keeps the door shut

A spring keeps the roller in the socket

Magnetic catches

Magnetic catches are not meant to hold strongly. They are used on such items as the doors of refrigerators and bathroom cupboards.

As the door is closed the magnet attracts the door plate and holds the door closed

The cupboard has a magnet in a frame screwed on the inside

The door has a steel plate screwed to the inside

A magnetic cupboard catch

Cutters

Cutting needs a specially-shaped edge and something to cut against. Knives and axes use one blade which is ground to a fine edge. Scissors, shears and pruners use two blades specially shaped to scrape, or shear, cleanly past each other.

The length of the handles controls how much pressure you can use to cut with.

Axe
An axe is like a giant knife. It has a blade that is sharpened on both sides to a fine edge.

The 'shoulders' of the blade get wider towards the handle. This wedge shape gives strength to the blade and makes chopping wood easier.

These power-driven sheep shears are worked by compressed air. The upper set of blades moves very quickly from side to side across the lower fixed set. Hairdressers clippers work in the same way

Pivot

8

Knife

A knife is a thin blade of steel and, like an axe, it has been carefully sharpened on both sides of one edge. Cutting is then a matter of pressing while pulling or pushing.

Secateurs are a garden tool that looks like a pair of scissors. Notice how the lower blade is curved and broad. This supports the stem or branch while the upper blade cuts cleanly through it

Scissors

Scissors have two blades that scrape past each other. If you look carefully you will see that each blade is half a wedge.

As the blades close they scrape against each other, squeezing, then **shearing**. Each blade has the inside face ground flat. The edge is almost square, but slopes away a little. This helps push the cut material apart.

This cross-section shows how the scissor blades close together. The wedge-shaped blades make the cutting edges

Single sloping face on each cutting edge

These large scissors are called pinking shears. They are, used to stop fabric from fraying while it is being sewed. Each blade is specially shaped to cut a wavy line

Locks

Lever lock

The projections on the key lift levers. If the key fits a lock it will lift all the levers together and the bolt will turn. The more levers there are to lift, the more secure the lock. This lock has only one lever. House locks usually have five levers.

A lock keeps doors and cupboards shut. Only those people with matching keys can unlock them.

A lock is a latch (see page 6) where the bar can only be lifted with the key.

There are two types of lock: one that uses a key that pushes in. This is called a cylinder or yale lock. The other type uses a set of levers. It is called a lever or mortice lock.

Materials to make a lock

Make a lever lock

You can make a lever lock key from a piece of dowel and a nail. You may need to ask a grown-up to help.

The key is made by hammering the nail a short way into the end of the dowel. To make the lock you need to cut a hole in a piece of board. The hole must be just the size to take the dowel/nail key.

On the back of the board you need to attach four short dowel pegs so that a strip of wood can slide between them. This is the bolt. The picture shows you the shape to cut in the 'bolt'. When you put the key through the hole you will be able to turn the nail so that it pushes the bolt.

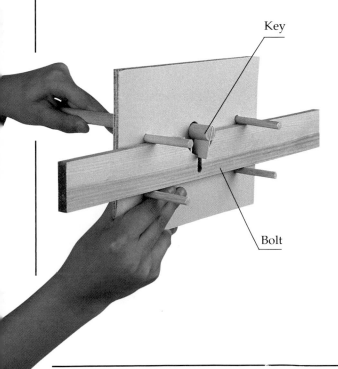

Key

Bolt

Keys for lever locks

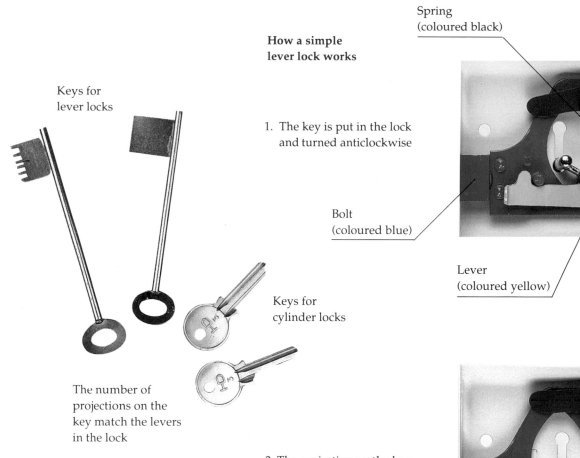

The number of projections on the key match the levers in the lock

Keys for cylinder locks

How a simple lever lock works

Spring (coloured black)

Bolt (coloured blue)

Lever (coloured yellow)

1. The key is put in the lock and turned anticlockwise

2. The projection on the key pushes the lever down out of the way and then begins to push the bolt

3. The key turns further and the bolt is fully out. See how the lever has risen behind the key to hold the bolt in place. The door is now locked

Cylinder lock

In a cylinder lock the bumps and dips of the key push up small pegs inside the lock. When you use the right key the pegs all line up and the key and cylinder can be turned. This pulls in the bolt and the door can be unlocked.

11

Openers

We often need to open cans and bottles. Here are some of the many devices for doing the job, and how they do it. Most of them work on the principle of levers.

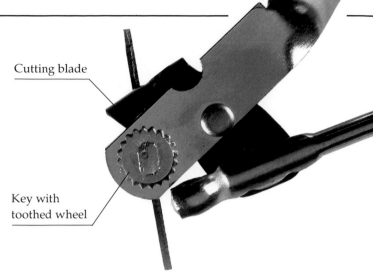

Cutting blade

Key with toothed wheel

Rotary can opener

The opener has a single blade that cuts into the metal of the can when the handles are squeezed together.

Once an opening has been made the key is turned. The toothed wheel digs into the outside of the can and pulls the blade through the can lid.

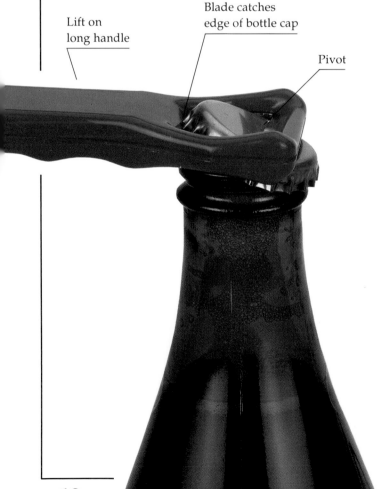

Lift on long handle

Blade catches edge of bottle cap

Pivot

Bottle opener

This opener fits over the cap of the bottle. A small lip fits down below the cap rim.

When you lift the handle two things happen: the lip pulls at the bottom of the cap and the small pip on the opener digs into the cap. The pip is the pivot.

As soon as the cap is half pulled off the seal breaks and the cap falls away.

The bent shape of the cap shows the way it was prised from the bottle. The crease shows where the pivot was placed

The handles are
squeezed together

Caution
Be careful of
sharp edges

Long handle to give
plenty of leverage

This piece pivots
on the can rim

Cutting blade

Lifting can opener

This can opener has no moving
parts. You have to bash the
pointed end into the tin and
so you need to be quite strong.
Once the blade has pierced the
can's lid you lift the handle.
This pulls the blade up against
the pivot and slices through the
can. You then push the blade
forward and repeat the action.

Key and tab openers

Some cans come with a key
and a slot. They are usually
very difficult to use because
you cannot get as much
leverage as with the other
types of opener.

Some of the hardest cans
to open are flat fish cans.
This picture shows a ring
pull tab on one corner. Try
to open one of these cans for
yourself. Can you see what
problems are caused? Can
you think of a better design?

Pens and pencils

Pens and pencils are used for writing. There are two different ways this happens. In pencils some of the solid is rubbed off by pressing hard; in pens the ink is drawn out of the pen by a ball, a piece of felt or a nib.

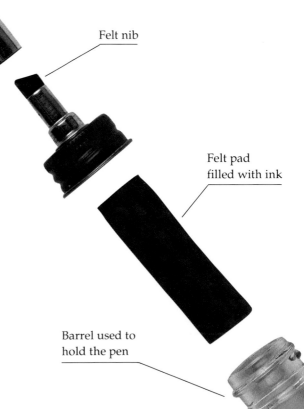

Ink is stored here

Nib opens to allow ink to flow

Fountain pens

Look closely at the nib of a fountain pen and you will see the ink just behind the tip. The ink is held in place by **surface tension**. When you press on the nib the two parts of it open out and provide a channel for the ink to flow down to the paper.

Felt nib

Felt pad filled with ink

Felt-tipped pens

These pens have a piece of 'felt', or fibre to make the nib. The ink is held inside the felt by surface tension in just the same way as water is held inside a sponge. (For more information on surface tension see *Science in our World, Volume 4, Water*).

When the fibre or felt tip is placed on the paper the porous surface of the paper pulls the ink into the paper.

Barrel used to hold the pen

Artists' pencils

Artists use pencils with many different colours. Their 'leads' are made from wax or other substances that have been dyed the chosen colour and then mixed with clay and resin.

Pencils

'Lead' pencils are not made out of lead, but a material called graphite. Graphite is a type of carbon, like soot and coal.

The graphite is powdered down and then mixed with clay and a type of glue called **resin**. This mixture sets hard into a long rod and is then glued inside a specially shaped wooden tube (the pencil).

When you press on paper, tiny flakes of graphite break away from the resin to leave a pencil mark.

Pencil leads vary in their hardness. Hard pencils have a large amount of clay mixed with the graphite and resin. Very soft pencils contain little clay.

Ball-point pens

These pens seem to have solid ink in them. In fact the ink has just been made very sticky so it won't run out of the barrel.

At the end of the barrel is a small ink tube and a ball. As you write the ball turns and rubs across the end of the ink tube, drawing off some of the ink. The ink is designed to dry immediately.

Roller ball

Sticky ink

Hooks and zips

A hook is a curved shape that is open and which can be used to latch onto things.

The hooks used on clothing are fairly easy to slip on and off, yet, unlike most hooks, they hold fast even when they are not being pulled.

Velcro's magic

Velcro® is used in strips in much the same way as zips. It is made of two parts. One part consists of looped material. The other part consists of thousands of tiny hooks.

When the two parts of the Velcro are brought together the hooks become caught up in the loops.

The springy nature of the plastic hooks makes sure they do not easily fall out. It also allows the hooks to be straightened when the Velcro is pulled apart.

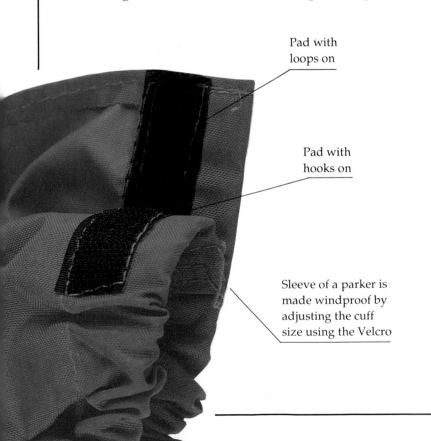

Pad with loops on

Pad with hooks on

Sleeve of a parker is made windproof by adjusting the cuff size using the Velcro

How a zip works

A zip is made from two rows of hooks tightly sewn into two strips of cloth. Each hook has a cup-shaped hollow on its back, so that hooks fit into the back of each other.

The zipper, or slide, is a small device that pushes the hooks together in such a way that the hooks and hollows mesh together tightly. The zipper's two channels draw the hooks together at a special angle, allowing the hook from one side to fit inside the cup on the back of the hook on the other side. Because the hooks are so close they cannot fall apart. Each hook holds the next one in place.

When the zipper is worked the other way, the wedge unclips all the hooks.

Wedge pushes the hooks apart when the zip is undone

Opened zip leaves this end

Channels bring the hooks together at a special angle when the zip is fastened

Closed zip leaves this end

Here the case of the slide has been cut away. Notice how the wedge fits between the hooks

Scales

Scales give accurate measurements of the weight of objects. They are used in shops, post offices, in the bathroom, the kitchen and for weighing out quantities in factories.

Many scales use springs to measure weight. Usually the springs are coils, but in some cases they are simply strips of springy metal.

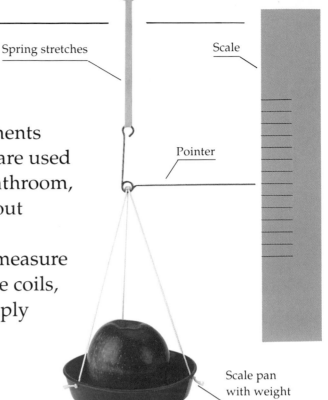

Spring stretches

Scale

Pointer

Scale pan with weight

A simple spring balance used by anglers for weighing fish. A pointer is connected to the bottom of the spring

(To find out more about how to make this spring scale see Science in our World, Volume 5, 'Falling')

A spring scale

Springs are coils of wire that get longer in proportion to the pull that is placed on them.

Simple spring scales are used to weigh fish after they have been caught.

A pointer is fixed to the lowest place on the spring. When an object is hung on the bottom of the spring it stretches and the pointer moves against a scale.

Kitchen scales

Many kitchen scales (the sort that do not need batteries) have a spring balance inside.

When you put food on the scale pan it stretches a tough piece of spring steel. To make the amount of stretching easier to see, the spring is fixed to a set of gear wheels that turn a small straight movement into a larger rotary one. The scale can now be placed round a disc as shown in the picture opposite.

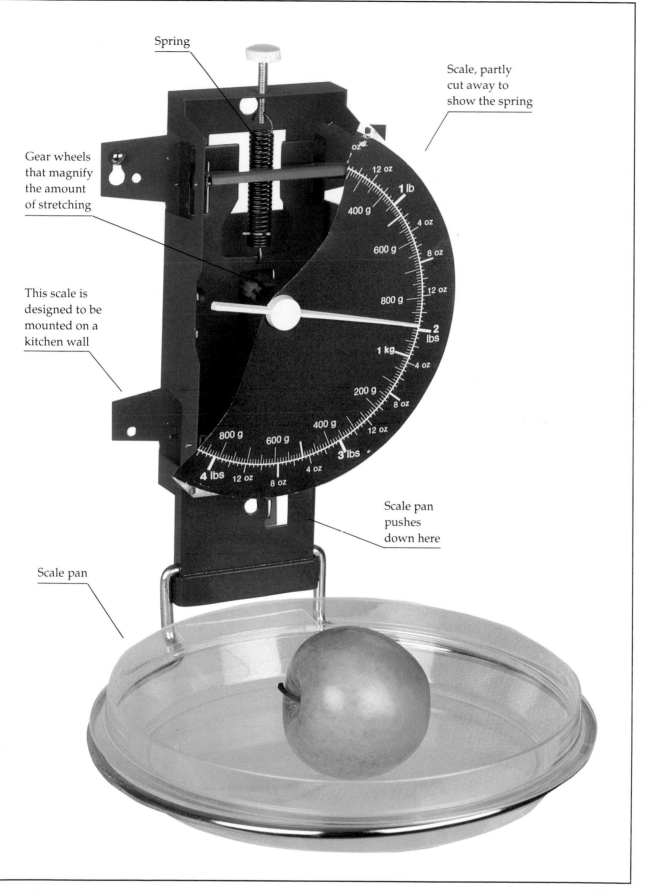

Spring

Scale, partly
cut away to
show the spring

Gear wheels
that magnify
the amount
of stretching

This scale is
designed to be
mounted on a
kitchen wall

Scale pan
pushes
down here

Scale pan

12 oz

1 lb

400 g

4 oz

600 g

8 oz

12 oz

800 g

2 lbs

1 kg

4 oz

200 g

8 oz

400 g

12 oz

800 g

600 g

3 lbs

4 lbs

12 oz

8 oz

4 oz

Sprays and jets

Water and other liquids can be turned into a spray by forcing them through very small holes. A mixture of these fine droplets and a gas, like air, is called an **aerosol**.

Sprays and jets have a variety of uses, for example to spray paint on cars, to water gardens, to apply polish to furniture and to make 'air-brush' pictures.

A spray bottle
Spray bottles have a big reservoir, a long thin tube that dips into the liquid, and a small nozzle (a type of hole) that is usually adjustable for size.

When the trigger is worked a plunger pushes air through the nozzle very quickly. This sucks liquid up the tube from the bottle.

As the liquid reaches the nozzle it is drawn through with the air. By twisting the outer part of the nozzle the hole can be made smaller – for a finer spray – or bigger for a coarser spray or a jet.

As spray bottles use air they do not harm the environment.

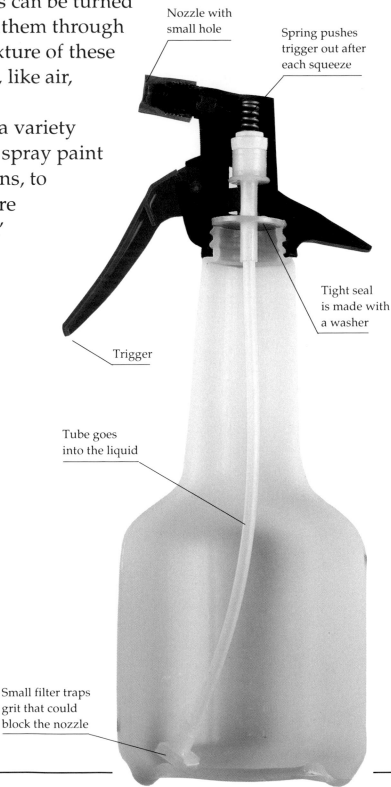

Nozzle with small hole

Spring pushes trigger out after each squeeze

Tight seal is made with a washer

Trigger

Tube goes into the liquid

Small filter traps grit that could block the nozzle

Aerosols

An aerosol can holds a gas under high pressure. When the nozzle is pressed the gas is released and drags some of the liquid with it. The liquid gets sprayed where it is needed; the gas disappears into the air.

Some gases (called CFCs) that have been used in aerosol cans may not be good for the environment. This is the reason it is best to use an air spray bottle rather than an aerosol can whenever possible.

Straw cut across and bent

Make an airbrush

Cut a piece of straw half through and bend it at an angle as shown here. Now dip one end in water and blow hard through the other. As you blow the air shoots across the lower part of the straw, sucking up water and making a spray. A narrow straw works more easily than a wide one. Artists often use this kind of spray for producing a very even finish.

21

Siphons

A siphon is a way of moving liquids from one place to another through a tube.

Irrigating fields, changing the water in fish tanks without disturbing the fish and flushing toilets are just some of the many uses for a siphon.

Make a siphon

To make a siphon you need a bowl with water in it and a length of plastic tube.

Put the whole plastic tube in the water until all the air has bubbled out. Put a finger over both ends to keep in the water. Still closing off both ends firmly, take one end of the tube out of the bowl and place it over an empty bowl. When you release both fingers water will pour from the upper bowl to the lower.

These tubes are siphoning water from the canal to irrigate the field

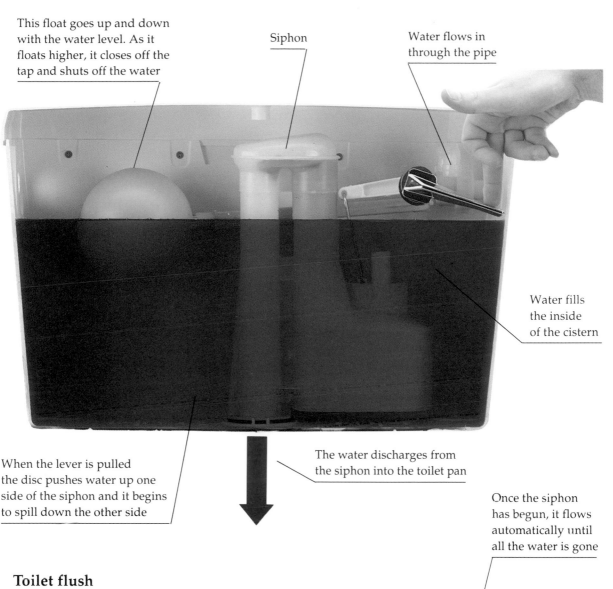

This float goes up and down with the water level. As it floats higher, it closes off the tap and shuts off the water

Siphon

Water flows in through the pipe

Water fills the inside of the cistern

When the lever is pulled the disc pushes water up one side of the siphon and it begins to spill down the other side

The water discharges from the siphon into the toilet pan

Once the siphon has begun, it flows automatically until all the water is gone

Toilet flush

Many automatic toilets use a siphon. Water flows into a reservoir called a cistern. As the cistern fills it raises a float which turns off the water. To flush the toilet the lever is pressed. This draws water up one arm of the siphon in the cistern and starts the siphoning action.

Water will be drawn out of the cistern until the level is low and air gets back into the siphon pipe. This system makes sure that enough water flows to flush the toilet thoroughly.

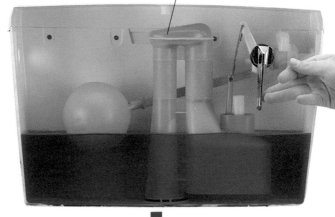

Binoculars

Our eyes need help to see distant objects such as birds in the tops of trees. Telescopes and binoculars are designed for seeing things a long way away.

Both telescopes and binoculars use **lenses**, small curved pieces of glass that bend light in special ways.

Here part of the binoculars has been cut away so you can see the prisms and lenses inside

The adjusting ring on the centre bar of the binoculars moves the eyepieces in and out of the tube to give the focus

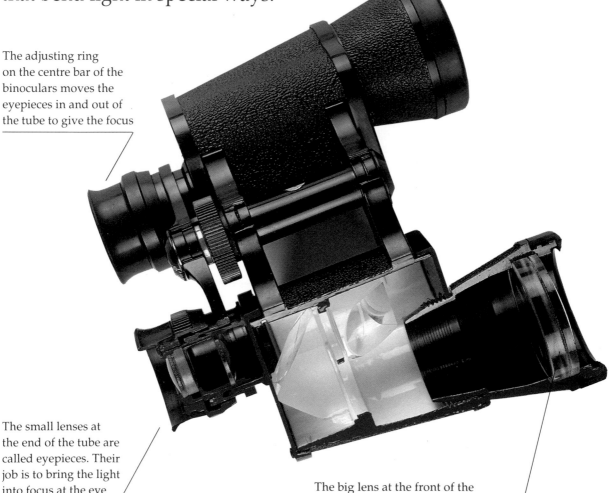

The small lenses at the end of the tube are called eyepieces. Their job is to bring the light into focus at the eye

(For more information on lenses and prisms, see Science in our World, Volume 6, 'Light')

The big lens at the front of the binoculars is called the objective lens. Its bulging shape gathers the light and sends it towards the eye. The size of the lens is very important. The bigger the lens the more light-gathering power it has

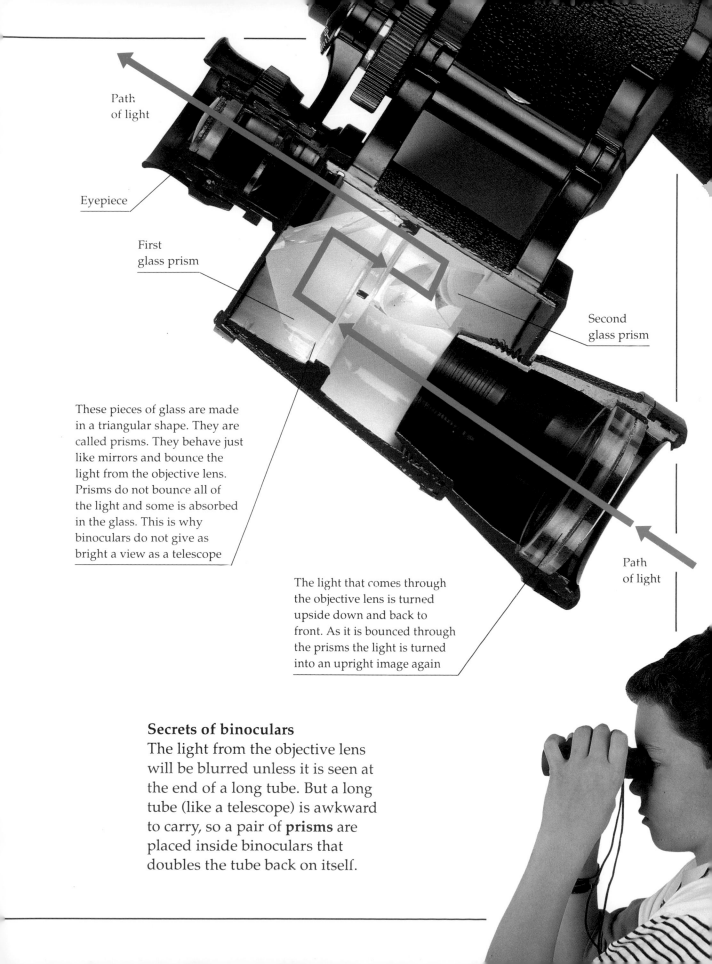

Path of light

Eyepiece

First glass prism

Second glass prism

These pieces of glass are made in a triangular shape. They are called prisms. They behave just like mirrors and bounce the light from the objective lens. Prisms do not bounce all of the light and some is absorbed in the glass. This is why binoculars do not give as bright a view as a telescope

The light that comes through the objective lens is turned upside down and back to front. As it is bounced through the prisms the light is turned into an upright image again

Path of light

Secrets of binoculars
The light from the objective lens will be blurred unless it is seen at the end of a long tube. But a long tube (like a telescope) is awkward to carry, so a pair of **prisms** are placed inside binoculars that doubles the tube back on itself.

Suckers

Small objects such as dust are very difficult to pick up. A **vacuum** cleaner creates a powerful draft or suction using a motor and a fan which pulls air and dust into a bag.

Vacuum machines are used as house cleaners, for filtering air in offices and factories. Scientists sometimes use a type of vacuum cleaner for collecting small insects for observation.

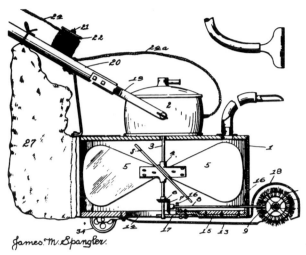

Original 'Hoover'
This picture shows the original patent design of the vacuum cleaner. It shows the sucking fan and the dust bag. The principle has not changed in 90 years.

Make a pooter
A pooter is a kind of vacuum cleaner that uses the suction created as you draw in your breath. You need a pair of straws and a jar with a tightly fitting lid.

On one of the straws you need to fit a small filter made from a piece of muslin.

The pooter is used by biologists to collect small insects from the surfaces of leaves, or out of water. The insects are not harmed by this process, whereas collecting them with tweezers might well crush them.

You can use your pooter to collect dust from a shelf or insects from water.

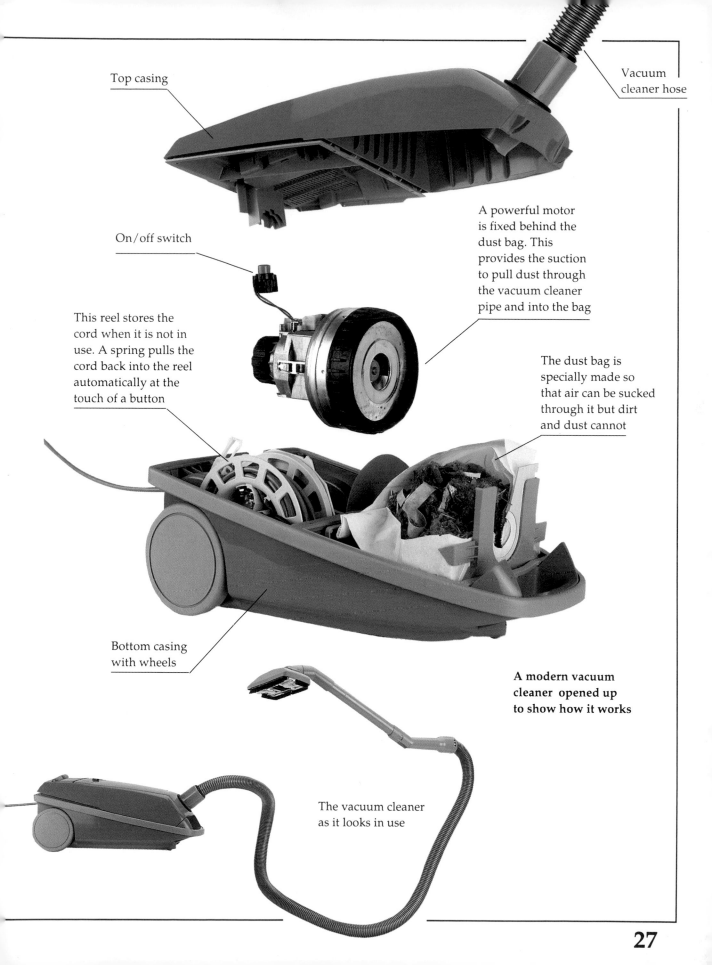

Top casing

Vacuum cleaner hose

A powerful motor is fixed behind the dust bag. This provides the suction to pull dust through the vacuum cleaner pipe and into the bag

On/off switch

This reel stores the cord when it is not in use. A spring pulls the cord back into the reel automatically at the touch of a button

The dust bag is specially made so that air can be sucked through it but dirt and dust cannot

Bottom casing with wheels

A modern vacuum cleaner opened up to show how it works

The vacuum cleaner as it looks in use

Calculators

Calculators are part of everyone's lives. Today we are used to handling small pocket calculators to add numbers and to do many more difficult tasks. But the principle of the calculator is very old; today's modern calculators are simply a fast way of doing the same job.

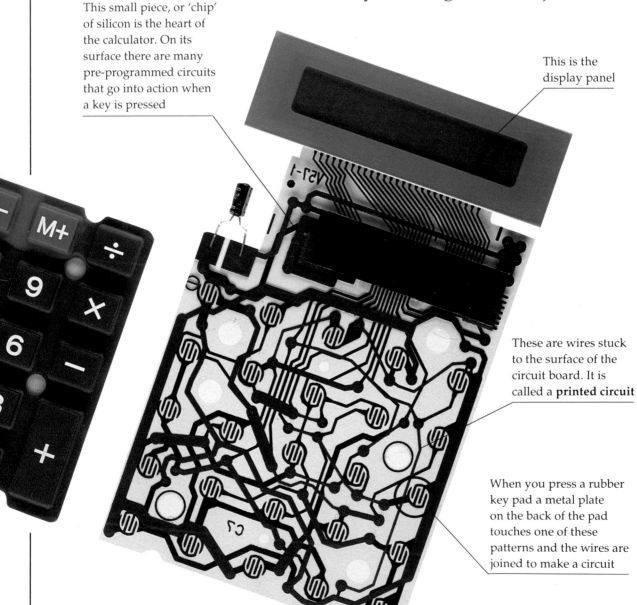

This small piece, or 'chip' of silicon is the heart of the calculator. On its surface there are many pre-programmed circuits that go into action when a key is pressed

This is the display panel

These are wires stuck to the surface of the circuit board. It is called a **printed circuit**

When you press a rubber key pad a metal plate on the back of the pad touches one of these patterns and the wires are joined to make a circuit

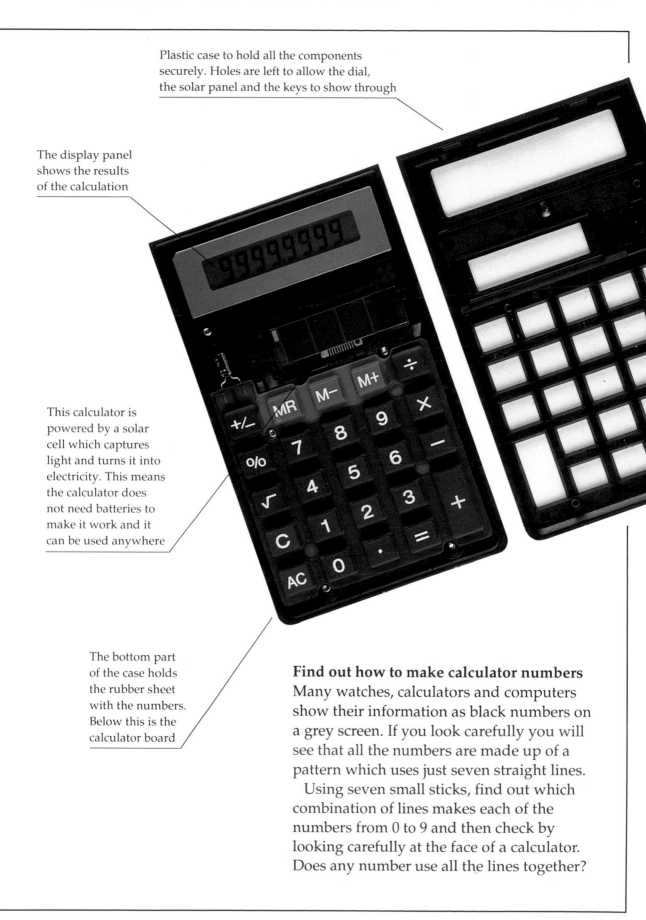

Plastic case to hold all the components securely. Holes are left to allow the dial, the solar panel and the keys to show through

The display panel shows the results of the calculation

This calculator is powered by a solar cell which captures light and turns it into electricity. This means the calculator does not need batteries to make it work and it can be used anywhere

The bottom part of the case holds the rubber sheet with the numbers. Below this is the calculator board

Find out how to make calculator numbers
Many watches, calculators and computers show their information as black numbers on a grey screen. If you look carefully you will see that all the numbers are made up of a pattern which uses just seven straight lines.

Using seven small sticks, find out which combination of lines makes each of the numbers from 0 to 9 and then check by looking carefully at the face of a calculator. Does any number use all the lines together?

Lifters and levers

We don't have the strength to do many of the things we want to, so we need machines to help us to be stronger and sometimes faster than we would normally be.

There are many ways of increasing what we can do, many of them by using long bars called levers.

The trolley

A trolley has wheels at the bend. To get the parcel off the ground the trolley is used as a lever. The wheels make a pivot. Because the handle is further from the pivot than the parcel, it is easy to lift it.

Once the weight of the parcel falls over the wheels, the person moving the trolley now only has to push the trolley, not lift the parcel as well.

Nutcrackers

The nutcracker has the pivot at one end. Notice how the nut is placed near the pivot and that the hand is at the end of long handles. This allows a tough nut to be cracked with relatively little effort.

Pivot

(For more information on how to do the experiment below see Science in our World, Volume 5, 'Falling')

How an ant can lift an elephant (in theory at least)

This model shows the principle of lifters and levers. Even a lightweight pencil sharpener can lift a heavy apple if the sharpener is placed a long way from the pivot, while the apple is placed close to it.

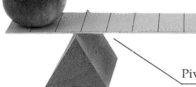

Pivot

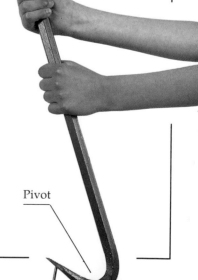

The crowbar

A crowbar is a steel rod bent close to one end. The short end is flattened so that it can be pushed under things that need lifting.

This bar is used for such things as opening cases that have been nailed down.

The bar is placed under the object and it is then pivoted about the bend. The long bar – the 'handle' – gives extra force.

Pivot

Turn of the screw

A screw is really a long sloping edge wound round a rod. The only way it can be moved is by twisting.

Many things are held together by screws – you will find them in chairs, tables and cupboards as well as taps and corkscrews. Sometimes they are hidden, so you may have to look hard.

Why bolts hold fast

A bolt is a screw that fits into another piece of metal. It is fitted through a hole and it is usually kept in place by something called a nut. The nut has a thread cut to match the thread on the bolt.

When they are tightened the thread on the bolt pulls hard against the thread on the nut. The harder it pulls, the tighter it becomes. This is the result of **friction**.

Taps

When you turn a tap you are turning a hidden screw. On the end of the screw is a rubber washer. As you turn the handle clockwise you screw the washer down over the hole that lets the water through. As you turn the handle anticlockwise you release the washer and allow the water to flow.

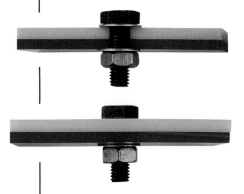

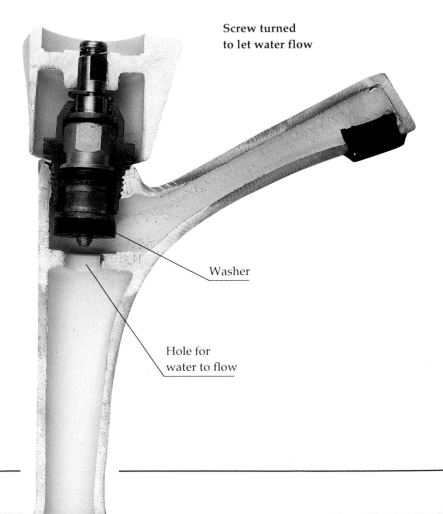

Screw turned to let water flow

Washer

Hole for water to flow

Corkscrew

A corkscrew is a way of getting a tightly fitting cork out of a bottle. Once the tip of the corkscrew has been pushed in the cork and twisted, it pulls itself into the cork.

Once the corkscrew is right inside the cork the handles can be used as a lever and the cork pulled out.

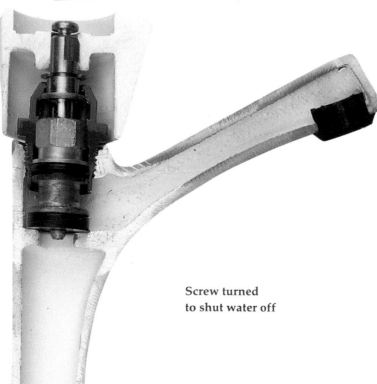

Screw turned to shut water off

Find out about friction

Friction is the 'stickiness' that develops when two objects are pulled or pushed across one another. It happens because all the tiny lumps and bumps of one surface catch against the lumps and bumps of the other. Even smooth surfaces would show lumps and bumps under a microscope.

To see how friction changes, put the palm of your hand down on a table. Now press on the table and push your hand forward. It moves in a jerky, slipping way.

If you press down with your other hand you make the frictional stickiness greater. See if you can press down so hard that you cannot move your hand at all.

Lamps

Without artificial light we would not be able to do very much at night. Many people in developing countries still burn wax, oil or paraffin. Today most modern lamps use electricity.

There are two kinds of electric lamp: those where electricity flows through a thin wire which gets very hot and glows; and those that make a gas-filled tube glow.

Light bulbs
Light bulbs use a special wire called a filament. Bulbs get very hot when they are working: they can even get hot enough to burn the skin. Because most of the energy is used in making heat these bulbs are not very efficient at giving out light.

However, filament bulbs are cheap to buy and they are used where lights are switched on and off a lot.

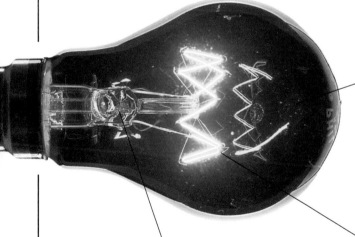

The bulb is filled with a gas called **argon**. This gas stops the filament from burning up

The wire is called a filament. It is made of a special metal that will not melt even when white hot

The filament is held up on a glass frame

1. The tube is filled with a special gas that sends out rays when electricity flows through it

2. The rays strike the coating in the inside of the tube

A paraffin lamp

This lamp is made in a developing world country using scrap metal. Paraffin is poured into the can and the wick and cap fitted.

Once the wick becomes wet it can be lit with a match. Paraffin lamps like this one burn with a sooty yellow flame.

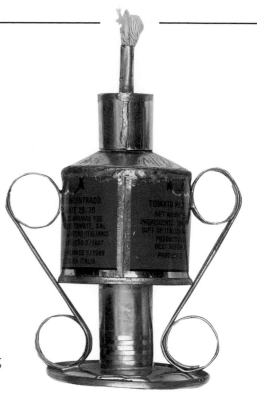

A fluorescent tube

If you look in the kitchen, in school or in an office or shop, you will often see long lighting tubes. These are called **fluorescent** tubes because on the inner surface of the tube is a special material which glows, or fluoresces, when special forms of light shine on it.

The tube is filled with a gas. When a high voltage is applied to the ends of a tube the gas allows electricity to pass through it. The flickering you see when a tube is first lit is made by the booster as it begins to discharge through the gas.

While electricity is flowing the gas gives out what is called **ultraviolet** light. We cannot see this light, but as it hits the coating on the inside of the tube it makes the coating glow and give out visible light.

Cheap to run

A fluorescent tube appears cool to the touch. This tells us that most of the energy is making light, not being wasted in making heat.

3. The coating glows. The colour you see varies with the substance used to coat the tube

These pieces make up the starting device. It produces a very high voltage and is enough to make electricity flow through, or discharge in, the gas in the tube

35

Making the connection

An electrical **circuit** only works when electricity can flow through it. However, it is often convenient to turn circuits on and off. Sometimes a simple plug and socket is all that is required; at other times a special switch is needed.

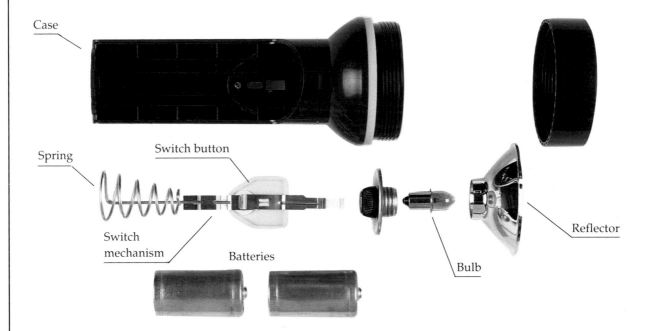

Case

Spring

Switch button

Switch mechanism

Batteries

Bulb

Reflector

This is the basic electrical circuit for a torch. A battery is connected to a bulb through a switch. *(For more information on electrical circuits, see* Science in our World, Volume 8, 'Electricity and Magnetism'*)*

How a torch works

One side of the battery is always held in contact with one contact of a bulb by a spring in the base of the case. The job of the switch is to connect the other end of the battery with the side of the bulb.

The switch on a torch is made of two long metal strips stretching from the spring to the reflector. When the switch slider is pushed towards the front of the torch the moving strip inside the case is pushed towards the bulb holder (which is also the reflector), completing the electrical circuit.

This is a type of
plug and socket
used in the USA

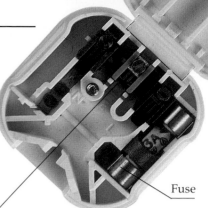

Colour codes in
the plug match the
colours of the cable.
(Not found on every
plug. Sometimes letter
codes are used)

Fuse

Electrical plugs

A plug is a kind of a switch
that you operate by pulling
the plug from the socket.

A socket has holes that are
connected to the electricity
supply. A plug has pins that
fit into the holes on the socket.
The wires leading to the plug are
colour coded to make sure they
are always connected properly.

A plug from
Australia

The switch

Many switches work by rocking
the switch lever, or toggle. When
the toggle is moved a projection,
or cam, on the underside of the
toggle pushes one piece of springy
metal down hard onto another
piece, making the connection.

The switch shown in this picture
is for low voltage use. However, in
a mains switch there is an
increased risk that the contacts will
spark and burn out as they close.
To get a quick make and break
action the toggle is spring loaded.
This is why all mains switches
spring between on and off
positions when they are operated.

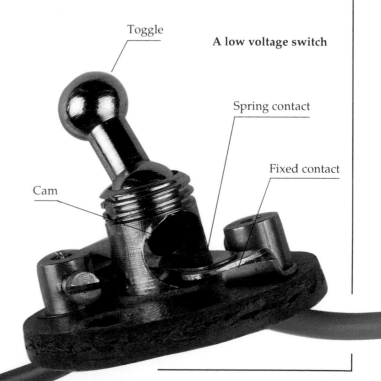

Toggle

A low voltage switch

Spring contact

Fixed contact

Cam

Bells, buzzers and chimes

Many front doors have some kind of bell, buzzer or chime. Fire alarms often use bells as warnings.

Each type of 'sounder' uses a magnet that rapidly switches on and off to make repeating sounds.

Chimes

Chimes are like bells and buzzers, but the bell is replaced by one or more pieces of metal, or chiming plate.

As the door bell switch is pressed electricity flows and moves an iron rod until it hits one of the metal chimes. When the door bell switch is released the rod rebounds and hits the second chime plate, giving a 'ding-dong' sound.

When the door bell switch is released, the magnetic effect stops and the spring throws the bolt back against the left hand striking plate. In this way you get two notes: 'ding–dong'

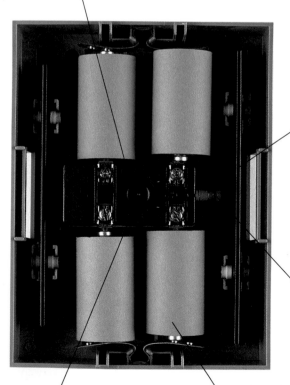

Chiming plate vibrates to give a pleasant sound when it is struck

When the coil becomes magnetised it throws this metal-cored bolt towards the right hand chime plate

The coil of wire that makes the magnet is in here

Batteries provide the electricity to work the chime

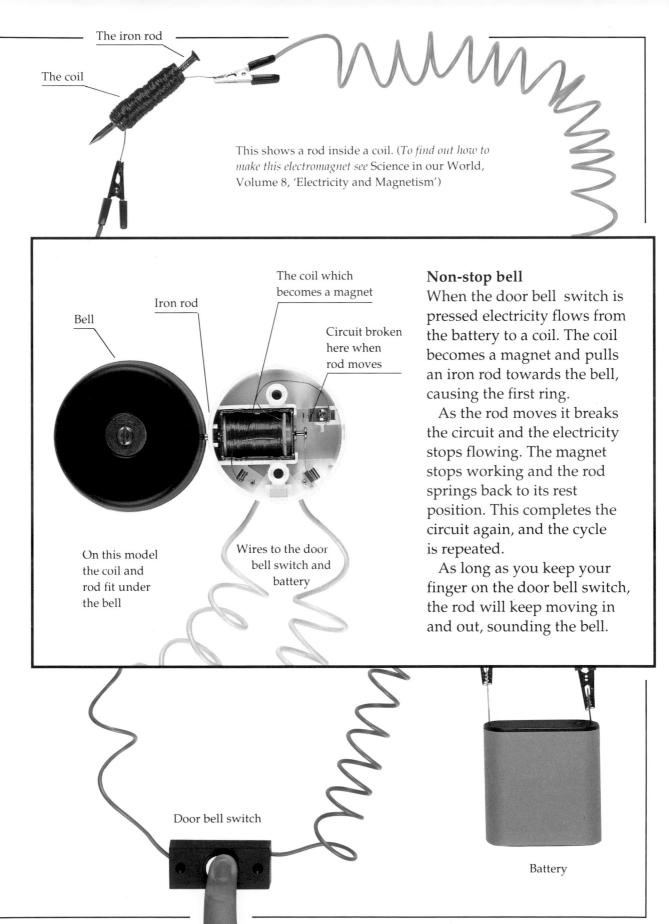

The iron rod

The coil

This shows a rod inside a coil. (*To find out how to make this electromagnet see* Science in our World, Volume 8, 'Electricity and Magnetism')

Bell

Iron rod

The coil which becomes a magnet

Circuit broken here when rod moves

On this model the coil and rod fit under the bell

Wires to the door bell switch and battery

Non-stop bell

When the door bell switch is pressed electricity flows from the battery to a coil. The coil becomes a magnet and pulls an iron rod towards the bell, causing the first ring.

As the rod moves it breaks the circuit and the electricity stops flowing. The magnet stops working and the rod springs back to its rest position. This completes the circuit again, and the cycle is repeated.

As long as you keep your finger on the door bell switch, the rod will keep moving in and out, sounding the bell.

Door bell switch

Battery

Refrigerators

Food keeps better when it is cold. A refrigerator is a machine that makes use of the way gases and liquids can carry heat.

The long tube on the outside is where the gas is compressed and gives out heat. This is why the tube at the back of a fridge gets hot

A traditional refrigerator with the feezing compartment at the top

What gases can do
When a gas is squeezed or compressed, it changes into a liquid. This squeezing 'wrings' a lot of heat out of the gas. When a squeezed liquid is allowed to expand back into a gas again, it soaks up a lot of heat from its surroundings. The trick is get the squeezing to happen outside the refrigerator, and the expanding inside it.

This is the compressor, an electric pump which pushes the gas round the system

Water's cooling power

You can see how cooling works by using a small square of paper kitchen towel and a thermometer.

Stand a thermometer in a room until it has had time to settle down. Write down the temperature.

Make the kitchen towel wet and loosely wrap it round the bulb of the thermometer. Within a few minutes the thermometer should read lower because heat has been taken out of the bulb as the water evaporated from the towel surface.

Cold gas moves along this pipe

The iced up surface of the freezer panel can clearly be seen

The freezer compartment is surrounded by the freezer panel to make sure the food stays icy cold

As the cold air from the ice box sinks down the fridge it gets into every corner

Arranging the food

The picture on the right shows a modern-style fridge-freezer. The left hand cabinet is a refrigerator and it has a cooling unit at the top. The air cools against this unit and then sinks to the bottom of the cabinet, keeping all the food cool. The right hand cabinet is a freezer and it has large cooling units in its sides. This keeps the food in all the drawers frozen.

Thermal flasks

It is very difficult to keep liquids very hot or very cold for more than a few minutes. This is because they soon share their heat with the surroundings.

A thermal flask slows down the sharing of heat and keep liquids hot or cold for hours. Here's how.

Wine cooler
Wine coolers are made of a double layer of plastic and work in the same way as thermal mugs, except that their job is to keep wine cool.

Thermal mugs
These mugs are designed to keep drinks hot. They are made of a double layer of plastic (which does not conduct heat easily). The air trapped between the layers is a good insulator, keeping the drinks in the mugs hot.

How a vacuum flask is made

The vacuum flask is the best kind of thermal flask. It can keep liquids hot or cold for many hours. It is basically a 'double-skinned' glass bottle.

A space without air or any other substance is called a **vacuum.** In a vacuum there is nothing to pass on the heat, so no heat can be lost or gained. The inner bottle of a vacuum flask is sealed to the outer one and nearly all the air is pumped out to make a vacuum

Glass is a strong material even when it is thin. It is easy to coat with silver and it does not take up or give out flavours to the liquids it contains

Silvering bounces back, or reflects, heat waves. The inside silvering on the vacuum flask reflects most of the heat back into the flask, keeping the liquid hot.
   The outer silvering bounces away any heat trying to get in to the flask. This is important when trying to stop a cold liquid from heating up

Plastic case to cushion against shocks

Heaters

It is very convenient to heat by electricity. You simply flick a switch and a kettle starts to boil, the toast begins to brown, or the room gets warm.

All heaters work in the same way. They have a special wire called an element which gets hot when electricity flows through it.

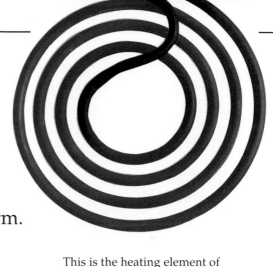

This is the heating element of an electric stove. Inside the insulated coil is a heating wire. When electricity flows the wire gets hot and this heats the outer case which then glows red hot

Caution
Never open
electrical appliances

A convector heater seen from the back with the panel removed. The heating element is near the bottom

Air is heated and flows out of the top

Cold air is drawn in from below

The convector heater
This silent heater is like a hair drier without the fan. The element is placed in a case which is shaped to make it work like a chimney. When electricity flows the element is heated and the heated air around the element rises. This sucks in cooler air from the bottom of the case.

The process of circulating heat is called **convection**.

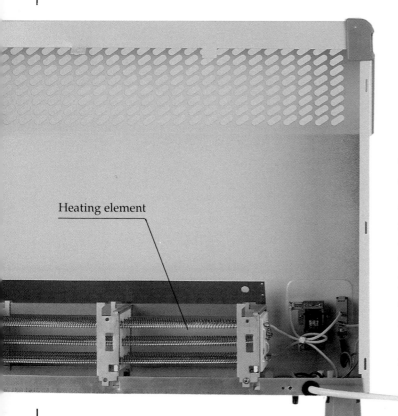

Heating element

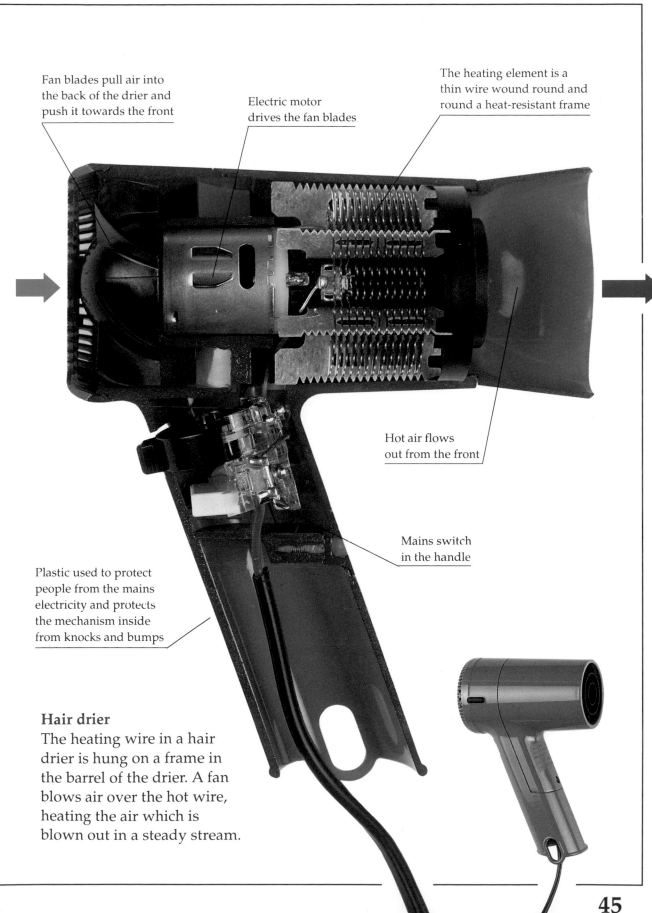

Fan blades pull air into the back of the drier and push it towards the front

Electric motor drives the fan blades

The heating element is a thin wire wound round and round a heat-resistant frame

Hot air flows out from the front

Mains switch in the handle

Plastic used to protect people from the mains electricity and protects the mechanism inside from knocks and bumps

Hair drier
The heating wire in a hair drier is hung on a frame in the barrel of the drier. A fan blows air over the hot wire, heating the air which is blown out in a steady stream.

New words

aerosol

an aerosol is a mixture of small particles, such as water or paint droplets, suspended in a gas such as air.

In a spray can the liquid that is to be made into particles is held under pressure with a gas. In the past the gases used were called CFCs. These gases are known to damage the environment.

Aerosol cans now have different gases in them, but a hand cranked spray will do many of the jobs that a pressure can will do and it does no damage to the environment because it uses air to force the liquid through the nozzle

argon

argon is a gas that makes up about one per cent of the air. It is called an inert gas, which means that it will not react with other substances easily. Argon is used in light bulbs or fluorescent lamps because it will not burn up when hot

circuit

a circuit is made of a number of electrical devices connected up in such a way that electricity flows through them. A circuit can be simple, as in the case of a torch, where a battery and a bulb are connected through a switch, or it might be very complicated, such as in a computer when tens of thousands of connections are involved

convection

this is a natural process that happens in a liquid or gas when they are heated or cooled. If a gas is made warmer it becomes lighter and starts to rise. If it gets cooler it becomes heavier and sinks. Air in contact with a heater rises as it warms. New air flows in to take its place and is warmed in turn. This sets up a flow of air or a current

friction

the resisting force that builds up between two objects when one of them is subject to a force such as turning or pushing. There is a limit to the friction that can oppose movement

fluorescent

the glowing effect that some coatings such as phosphor give out when they are struck by ultra-violet light. Fluorescent tubes use four or five times less energy than an ordinary bulb for the same light output

lens

this is a piece of transparent material that is used to change the size of things we look at. There are two common types of lens. In the kind called convex, the lens magnifies. You can recognise it because it has bulging sides. In the type of lens called concave the lens makes things smaller. This lens has dished sides

magnetic

a material is magnetic when it has the ability to attract iron objects to it. Magnets have places where their magnetic effect is concentrated called magnetic poles. In a magnetic catch the pole of a magnet is placed so that it faces the strip of iron on the door

pivot

a point about which an object can turn. For example the shaft and hub of a bicycle wheel is a pivot for the wheel

printed circuit

this is a pattern of connections that are made in many pieces of electronic equipment. All the connecting wires are made of flat strips of metal which are stuck down onto a base board. Because they are fixed down there is less chance of mistaking the connections or of the wires breaking

prism

the name of a triangular-shaped piece of transparent material, usually glass. Its sides are cut at an angle of 45 degrees. When light enters a prism it is turned back on itself. Prisms are used in binoculars to shorten the length of the sighting tubes

resin

this is a material rather like glue that comes from trees

shearing

a tearing type of action that happens when two blades close on a material like paper

surface tension

the way that some liquids such as water behave in the presence of air by having the appearance of an elastic skin. Surface tension keeps water droplets whole instead of spreading out as a film

ultraviolet light

this is part of the wide range of light that comes from the Sun. We can only see part of the Sun's radiation. This is called visible light. The type of radiation that is out of our visual range and just beyond violet is called ultraviolet

vacuum

this is the absence of air. A vacuum exists in space but a near vacuum can be made for certain special reasons. The most common near vacuum is found in thermal flasks and in television tubes. If one of these containers is broken the air rushes in and gives the effect of an explosion, scattering pieces of sharp glass. It is therefore dangerous to break vacuum flasks

Index